THE LITTLE BOOK OF
Bathroom
Brainteasers

THE LITTLE BOOK OF

Bathroom Brainteasers

NO PENCILS REQUIRED!

head-scratching puzzlers for every day

NATHAN HASELBAUER

FAIR WINDS

PRESS

GLOUCESTER, MASSACHUSETTS

Text © 2004 by Nathan Haselbauer

First published in the USA in 2004 by
Fair Winds Press
33 Commercial Street
Gloucester, MA 01930

08 07 06 05 04   1 2 3 4 5

ISBN 1-59233-102-5

Library of Congress Cataloging-in-Publication Data available

Series cover design by Peter King & Company
Book design by *tabula rasa* graphic design

Printed and bound in Canada

This book is dedicated to all the people out there who have never stopped learning.

Acknowledgments

This book would have been all but impossible to compile and write without the help of the International High IQ Society. The members of the society are some of the best brainteaser aficionados around, and their help was invaluable when it came time to think of new brainteasers and to make sure the ones I wrote had the correct answers.

INTRODUCTION

This book contains a rich selection of 201 brainteasers—from math and logic problems to word games. All of them are extremely short—you should be able to solve most of them in your head in just a minute or two! You won't need an advanced mathematical background to figure them out. All you need is an active intelligence and an inquisitive mind. You'll find the answers at the back of the book—but don't look! So put on your thinking cap, get started, and some have brainteasin' fun!

1

When Peter and Bill ran a 100-meter race,
Peter won by five meters. To give Bill a
chance to win, they raced again, but this time Peter
started five meters behind the starting line.

Each man ran the race at the same
speed as in the first race.

What were the results of the second race?

2

Little Billy bought a pack of baseball cards and found a rookie card worth $10. He decided to sell it to his friend Tommy for $10. After the baseball season ended, the card was worth more and Billy bought it back from Tommy for $15. The following year, Billy sold the card for $8. Did Billy make or lose money in the end?

?

3

A teacher told her students, "I have a bag of lollipops that I bought for $6.25. Can anyone figure out how many are in the bag and how much I paid for each one?" The students looked puzzled and said there's no way anyone could know how many lollipops were in the bag.

The teacher said, "The lollipops were all the same price. The number I bought is the same as the number of cents each cost." Can you figure out how much the lollipops cost?

?

4

Tricia, Kelly, Sasha, and Meredith started a book club that will meet once a month. Each month, one person hosts the party and another person brings the snacks. The host gets to pick the book and one of the other three has to bring the snacks. The responsibility of the host and the provider of snacks changes every month. How many months will it take until there has been every possible combination of host and snack-provider?

5

The New York City subway system buys wheels for their subway cars for $200 per wheel. The wheels last for ten years and then they have a scrap value of $25 apiece. If rust-proofing treatment costing $50 a wheel is applied, each wheel will last fifteen years but will have no scrap value. In the long run, would it be more cost effective to rust-proof the wheels or not?

?

6

Ian and Adam wanted to go to Coney Island and were trying to figure out the fastest way to get there. Ian wanted to take the subway, but Adam noted that the subway only gets halfway to Coney Island and then you have to walk the rest of the way. Adam said the fastest way to get there would be by bicycle, but Ian still felt the subway would be faster. So Adam hopped on his bicycle and Ian took the subway. The subway was four times as fast as Adam on his bicycle, but Adam was twice as fast as Ian's walking speed. Who got to Coney Island first?

7

After graduating from college, Alison went to work for a financial firm and Eric went to work for a law firm, both earning the same amount. Last year, Alison had a raise of ten percent and Eric had a drop in pay of ten percent. This year, Alison had a ten percent drop in pay and Eric had the ten percent raise. Who is making more now, or are they getting paid the same?

?

8

Both Aaron and Alexander are average marksmen and only hit their target fifty percent of the time. They decide to fight a duel in which they exchange alternate shots until one is hit. What are the odds that the man who shoots first will hit the other?

9

If Beth is as old as Bill will be when Trish is as old as Beth is now, who is the oldest?

10

A rowboat is floating in a swimming pool.
Will dropping a marble in the pool or in the rowboat
raise the level of the water in the pool higher?

11

What is the largest amount of money you can have in
coins and still not be able to give change for a dollar?

12

Patti and John decided to play squash against each other, betting ten dollars on each game they played. Patti won three games and John won $50. How many games did they play?

13

On a digital clock, how many times in a twelve-hour period are the numbers displayed in consecutive order (for example, 1:23)?

14

At the annual high-school baked goods sale, Mrs. Ramsey sold sixty pies during the six-day sale. Each day, she sold four more pies than she did on the previous day. How many pies were sold on the first day?

?

The local high school was trying to raise money for a class trip by having students pay $1 to guess the number of jellybeans in a jar. Adam guessed there were forty-three, Bill guessed thirty-four, and Carl guessed forty-one. One person was off by six, another was off by three, and another was off by one. How many jellybeans were in the jar?

?

16

A banker had a scale that was only balanced when there were three gold bars on one side of the scale and one gold bar and a ten kilogram weight on the other side. Assuming all the gold bars weigh the same amount, how much does one gold bar weigh?

?

17

Steve and Lisa each have a bag containing the same number of marbles. How many marbles must Steve give Lisa so that Lisa will have ten more marbles than Steve?

18

There were four men in the lobby waiting to interview for the same job. They shook hands with each other just once. How many handshakes were made?

Under the Christmas tree there were three presents—
one for Samantha, one for Maria, and one for Louisa.
Each present was wrapped with a different color paper, either
red, green, or silver. There was also a different color bow
on each present, either red, green, or gold. Using only the
following two statements, determine the color of wrapping
paper and bow that was on each of the presents.

1. Samantha's present had a green bow.
2. Louisa's present was the only one without contrasting
colors of bow and paper.

?

20

The Moore family had twelve people over for candied apples but they only made seven apples. How did they divide the seven candied apples so that everyone had equal portions? Each apple cannot be cut into more than four pieces.

21

Mary Ellen and Barbara both have gardens of equal size in their front yard. Barbara decides to plant a single weed in Mary Ellen's garden so it won't look as nice. The weed doubles every day, and within thirty days Mary Ellen's garden is completely covered in weeds. If we assume the weed doubles in number every day, how many days will it take Barbara's garden to be completely covered in weeds when Mary Ellen plants two weeds in her garden?

?

22

If each of Peter's sons have twice as many sisters as brothers and each of his daughters have just as many sisters as brothers, how many sons and daughters does Peter have?

23

If the minute hand had just passed the hour hand, how long would it take until the next time this happens?

?

24

A cereal company is offering a magic decoder ring
to anyone who sends in enough box tops. Jess and
Courtney both want a ring, but Jess needs seven
more box tops and Courtney needs one more.
They thought of combining their box tops to get
one ring, but they still don't have enough.
How many box tops are needed for one ring?

?

Trish decided to go on a shopping spree.
At the shoe store, she spent half of what she had
plus $6 for a pair of boots. At the clothing store, she spent
half of what was left plus $4 for a scarf. At the
candy store, she spent half of what remained plus
$2 for an ice cream cone. She had $7 left over.
How much did she have originally?

26

There are nine jars, each containing a different type of liquid, but the labels have all fallen off. Knowing nothing about the contents, a passerby reapplies the labels at random. What is the expected number of correctly labeled jars?

?

27

A single-elimination billiards tournament is held for 100 players. How many matches will be played before a winner is crowned?

28

If 1,000 gumballs cost $20, how much would ten gumballs cost?

29

A weightless and perfectly flexible rope is hung
over a weightless, frictionless pulley attached to the roof
of a building. At one end is a weight that exactly
counterbalances an orangutan at the other end.
If the orangutan begins to climb, what will
happen to the weight?

?

Jimmy practices playing the piano one hour a day from Monday through Friday. How many hours must he practice on Saturday in order to have an average of two hours a day for the six-day period?

31

On a busy night, the valet parked 320 cars.
Twenty-one percent of the customers tipped him $1,
half of the remaining seventy-nine percent
tipped him $2, and the rest did not tip at all.
How much money did the valet make?

Trish was looking in her closet, trying to figure
out how many handbags she owned. All her
bags are gold except two. All her bags are
brown except two. All her bags are white except two.
How many handbags does Trish have?

33

At the office party, Tommy and Ally were planning on handing out jellybeans. They were hungry, however, and Tommy had already eaten half of the jellybeans when Ally ate half the remaining jellybeans plus three more. There were no jellybeans left. How many jellybeans did they take to the office party?

?

34

A car dealer spent $20,000 for some used cars.
He sold them for $27,500, making an average of $1,500
on each car. How many cars did he sell?

35

Dan and Craig were playing pool for $1 a game.
At the end of the day, Dan won $4 and Craig won three
times. How many games did they play?

?

36

If Bill is taller than Mick and shorter than John,
who is the tallest of the three?

37

Danielle is now as old as Kelly was eight years ago. Who is older?

38

Mary Ellen was having a garage sale and someone came by and bought the lawnmower. The person paid $100 for it and paid with a check. Before leaving, he decided he didn't want the lawnmower; he wanted the $75 chainsaw instead. Mary Ellen gave the person $25 change and he left. The check later bounced, and she was charged a $25 fee by the bank. If the chainsaw originally cost her $50, how much did she lose?

39

During naptime, Juan was sleeping between Miguel and
Enriqué. Ricardo was sleeping on Enriqué's right.
Who was Enriqué sleeping between?

40

Tom sells desks and chairs. The desks cost twenty-five times as much as the chairs do. Tom sold ten items, and one-fifth of them were desks. If the desks cost $100 for two, how much money did Tom earn?

Toby was an eccentric man who decided to give his fortune away to the winner of a horse race. In the rules, the winner was the one who came in last. Toby didn't want the race to last forever, so he came up with an idea to prevent the jockeys from deliberately riding slowly to place last. What was Toby's idea?

42

How many times does the minute hand pass the hour
hand between noon and midnight on a normal clock?

43

Is it possible for Peggy to have seven children if
half of them are girls?

44

At the local shopping mall, Stephen went
into five stores, eventually spending all his money.
In each store, he spent $1 more than half of what he
had when he came in. How much money did Stephen
have when he went into the first store?

?

45

Every hour on the hour a train leaves Austin for Dallas and a train leaves Dallas for Austin.

The trains all travel at the same speed and the trip from Austin to Dallas takes five hours. How many trains pass by each other on one trip?

46

While running a 3,000-meter race on an indoor track, Joseph notices that one-fifth of the runners in front of him plus five-sixths of the runners in back of him add up to the total number of runners. How many people are running in the race?

47

The director of an orphanage wanted to get a present for all the kids who didn't already have every toy. The orphanage has 100 kids: eighty-five have a bicycle, seventy-five have a baseball glove, seventy have a cowboy hat, and eighty have toy soldiers. What is the least possible number of kids who own a bicycle, baseball glove, cowboy hat, and toy soldiers?

For an international summit, fifteen representatives from the United States, France, Britain, and Germany met in Switzerland. Each country sent a different number of representatives and each country is represented by at least one person. Britain and France sent a total of six representatives. France and Germany sent a total of seven representatives. Which country sent four representatives?

49

Bill and Lorraine are preparing to take a 4,000-mile trip in their car. The car has four tires and each tire lasts only 1,500 miles. How many tires will Bill and Lorraine go through if we assume the tires on the car are brand new?

?

50

Jess is planning on running the Boston marathon and the New York City marathon. Jess finds a store that has sneakers on sale and she wants to buy enough sneakers to get through both marathons. If each marathon is twenty-six miles and each pair of sneakers lasts ten miles, how many pairs of sneakers should Jess buy?

Three people are having a dinner party. Blake shows up with five dishes and his friend Brian brings three dishes. Jodi stops by with no dishes but decides to sit down and eat with them. Jodi pays $20 as her share. If we assume that all the dishes have the same value, how can the $20 be split between Blake and Brian?

?

52

In the barnyard there are goats and chickens.

In all, there are 22 heads and 72 feet.

How many chickens and goats are there in the barnyard?

Chris is on a ladder painting a wall. He starts
on the middle rung, goes up six rungs, goes down eight
rungs, up three rungs, and up twelve more rungs to
reach the top bar of the ladder. How many rungs
are there on the ladder?

Angela is interviewing for new jobs and has narrowed it down to two possible companies. The first company offers $27,000 per year with a $1,000 per year raise given twice a year. The second company is also offering $27,000 with a $2,000 per year raise given once a year. Which job should Angela choose?

55

A sushi restaurant buys twenty fish for $10 each. The owner knows that fifty percent of the fish will go bad before being served. Each fish creates ten servings. What price must they charge per serving in order to make a one hundred percent profit on their initial investment?

56

Eric decides to climb Mt. Everest with the help of Sherpas. It will take him six days to reach the summit, but he can only carry four days' worth of food in his pack. If the Sherpas can also only carry four days' worth of food, how many Sherpas will Eric need to reach the summit?

?

57

You are in a strange country that uses a currency system you've never seen before. In your pocket you have only seven-cent coins and eleven-cent coins. What is the most expensive item that cannot be purchased with any combination of the two coins?

Tommy goes to the bank to cash his $1,500 paycheck, but the bank is out of certain bills. The teller cashes Tommy's check using a certain number of $1 bills and ten times as many $5 bills, and a certain number of $10 bills and twice as many $50 bills. How many bills of each kind does the teller pay out?

59

Courtney was selling pieces of candy at the fair
and ended up with $2.46 in change. She has the same
number of pennies, nickels, dimes, and quarters.
How many of each does she have?

?

Elena decided to run twenty miles to warm up
for the marathon. She ran the first half at five-miles-per
hour and ran the second half at ten-miles-per hour.
What was her average speed?

61

You are given five identical sacks containing ten gold coins each. All the gold coins weigh one pound each, except for the coins in the fifth sack. In the fifth sack, all the gold coins weigh nine-tenths of a pound.

How can you figure out which sack has the lighter coins in it using a single-tray scale if you are only allowed to use the scale once?

62

During spring training, Derek and Bernie were practicing hitting balls. His first time at bat, Derek hit seventy-five out of a hundred pitches. Then Bernie hit seventy-five out of a hundred pitches. On Derek's second turn at bat, he hit thirty-five of the fifty pitches thrown. Bernie didn't take a second turn at bat. Who had the best average for the day—Derek or Bernie?

?

63

Little Tricia is playing with blocks in her room. She decides to stack up all the blocks so that each row has one less block than the row below. Tricia has fifty-five blocks total and she wants to end up with just one block on top. How many should she put on the bottom row?

?

One cup of green tea has twenty-five percent more caffeine than one cup of coffee. If Greg drinks five cups of coffee and Tim drinks four cups of green tea, who drank more caffeine?

All of Alison's pets are cats except one. All of her pets are goldfish except one. How many cats and goldfish does Alison have?

At LaGuardia Airport there are three clocks in the terminal. Clock A says it's 8:00, clock B says it's 8:50, and clock C says it's 8:20. One of the clocks is twenty minutes fast, one is slow, and one is off by half an hour. What is the actual time?

67

It takes seventeen minutes for seventeen bakers to bake seventeen cookies. How many bakers do you need to bake fifty-one cookies in fifty-one minutes?

?

The cat named Coco is heavier than the
cat named Lulu. Winston weighs more than Fluffy
but less than Rocky. Fluffy weighs more than Lulu.
Rocky weighs less than Coco.
List the cats in the order of their weights,
starting with the heaviest.

71

A new brand of oatmeal cookies has ninety percent less fat than the regular brand. How many of the reduced fat cookies would I have to eat to ingest the same amount of fat that would be in one regular oatmeal cookie?

?

72

Jackie was walking down the street and found $4 on the sidewalk. She put the $4 in her purse with the money she had before she found it and she now had five times the amount of money she would have had if she had lost $4. How much money did Jackie have before she found the $4?

Sammy has fifty coins in his pocket that add up to one dollar.
How many coins of each denomination are in Sammy's pocket?

A snail is at the bottom of a ten-foot well. He climbs
three feet a day, but during the night, while resting,
he slips back two feet. At this rate, how many days will it
take the snail to climb out of the well?

75

Jean-Pierre opened his first French cooking class, and he has fewer than 500 students. One-third of the students is a whole number. So are one-fourth, one-fifth, and one-seventh of the students. How many students are enrolled in Jean-Pierre's cooking class?

76

Beth is twice as old as her brother and half as old as her father. In 22 years, her brother will be half as old as his father. How old is Beth now?

77

If you have a group of six-legged flies and eight-legged spiders and there are forty-eight legs in total, how many flies and how many spiders are there in the group?

Andy, Bill, Chris, Drake, and Eric are mice learning to go through a maze. Each time a mouse reaches the end of the maze, it gets a pellet of food.

So far, Andy has gotten four more pellets than Bill. Bill has gotten seven fewer pellets than Chris. Chris has gotten five more pellets than Drake, and Drake has gotten three more pellets than Eric. Bill and Drake have gotten ten pellets between them. How many times has each mouse gone through the maze so far?

79

Jack has six brothers. Each brother is four years
older than his next younger brother. The oldest brother
is three times as old as his youngest brother.
How old are each of the brothers?

80

Using pennies, nickels, dimes, and quarters,
how many of which coins should I give you if you
want one dollar in twenty-eight coins?

81

Two people can make two hats in two hours. How many
people are needed to make twelve hats in six hours?

?

82

Kelly went to the candy store and was able to buy exactly 100 pieces of candy for a dollar. Some of her candy cost ten cents a piece; some of her candy cost three cents a piece; and some of her candy cost one cent for two pieces. How many pieces of each kind of candy did Kelly buy?

?

83

Anthony, Bill, Carl, and Dave all decided to start taking
singing lessons. Carl took twice as many lessons as Bill.
Anthony took four lessons more than Dave but three
fewer than Carl. Dave took fifteen lessons altogether.
How many singing lessons did Bill take?

84

Patricia loves her shoes. She has ten pairs of shoes in five different colors. Patricia is a particularly lazy person, however, and just tosses her shoes in a bin when she takes them off. She needs to go away for a weekend on business, but she put off packing until really early in the morning. It's still dark outside and she can't see the color of the shoes in the bins. How many individual shoes will she have to take out of the bin to be sure that she has at least two of the same color?

?

85

John went to Mexico and bought a painting for $2,500. When he came home, his friend Lance saw the painting and gave John $3,500 for it. A few days later, John bought the painting back for $4,500, thinking it would be worth more someday. He took it to an art dealer, who offered him $5,500 for it, so John sold it to the art dealer. Did John make money or lose money in the end?

?

Dan's weekly salary is $70 less than Jerry's, whose weekly salary is $50 more than Sally's. If Sally earns $280 per week, how much does Dan earn per week?

?

Juanita loved to put jigsaw puzzles together.
She managed to try at least one puzzle per day.
For every puzzle she completed, she gave herself two
points, and for every puzzle she couldn't complete, she
subtracted three points. After thirty days of putting
together puzzles, Juanita had a score of zero.
How many puzzles was she able to complete?

88

Patti moved to Seattle and wasn't used to all the rain.
She decided to make a rain gauge to measure the
amount of rain for one week. It rained each day
that week, starting on Monday, and each day the
amount of rain in the gauge doubled. By the following
Sunday, the rain gauge was completely filled.
On which day was the rain gauge half-filled?

?

89

A car dealership reduced the price of one of its models by twenty five percent for its Year End Sale. By what percentage of the sales price must it be increased to put the car back to its original price?

90

Using pennies, nickels, dimes, and quarters, how many of which coins should I give you if you want one dollar in six coins?

Brian decided to propose to Andrea and went shopping for a ring. At the first jewelry store, he found a one-carat ring for $3,000. At the second jewelry store, he found the same one-carat ring for $3,500. The first jewelry store had a twenty percent fee for any rings that were returned and the second jewelry store had no fees for returns. If there is a fifty percent chance that Andrea will say no, which jewelry store should Brian buy the ring at to maximize his risk/reward?

During a summit meeting, John is in charge of protecting two diplomats, one from France and one from Britain. John has a twenty-five percent chance of thwarting an assassination attempt against the French diplomat and a fifty percent chance of thwarting an assassination attempt against the British diplomat. If there are six people at the summit who are going to attempt to assassinate the French diplomat and ten people attempting to assassinate the British diplomat, which diplomat is in greater danger of being assassinated?

93

Michael had a job at the produce stand stacking oranges.
His boss told him to stack thirty-five oranges so
that each row of oranges would have one more than
the row above it. How many rows of oranges did
Michael have when he was finished?

94

There is a flagpole in the middle of Lake Tahoe. Half of the flagpole is in the lake bed, another one-third of it is covered by water, and ten feet of the flagpole is sticking out of the water. What is the total length of the flagpole?

95

At Longmeadow High School, everyone plays on a sports team. There are five more soccer players than baseball players. There are three more students on the track team than on the baseball team. There are two more football players than hockey players. There are three more students on the track team than on the football team. The number of baseball and football players equals eight. How many players are on each team?

?

96

It takes Mary one hour to install carpet on a bedroom floor that is nine-feet wide and twelve-feet long. How long will it take her to put carpet on the living room floor, which is twice as wide and twice as long?

97

The local high school has an annual tug-of-war game between the sports players. With three football players on one side and two baseball players on the other side, the game ended in a tie. Similarly, with three soccer players on one side and four baseball players on the other side, the game ended in a tie. Which side, if either, will win if one side has five football players and the other side has two soccer players?

?

98

Vince drove to from Atlantic City to New York at the rate of twenty miles an hour. When he got to New York, he realized he forgot his wallet and rushed home at forty miles an hour. The whole trip took him six hours. How many miles is it from Atlantic City to New York?

99

Tommy and Ralph both own clothing stores selling the same items. Tommy sells the same pair of shoes as Ralph, and they both sell for $100. Tommy decides to lower the price by twenty-five percent and Ralph counters by lowering the price thirty percent. When Tommy finds out that Ralph lowered the price on his shoes, Tommy lowers the price of his by another fifteen percent. Ralph in turn lowers the price of his by ten percent. Who is selling the shoes for less?

?

100

Carlos is playing roulette in Las Vegas.
If there are thirty-six numbers on the wheel,
figure out which two-digit number Carlos has
placed his bet on, given the following facts:

The number is divisible by three.

The sum of the digits in this number
lies between four and eight.

It is an odd number.

When the digits in this number are multiplied
together, the total lies between four and eight.

At the MegaloMart wholesale shopping market they sell large containers of orange juice and apple juice.

On the shelves there are six containers,
each holding the following amounts:
Container A: thirty quarts
Container B: thirty-two quarts
Container C: thirty-six quarts
Container D: thirty-eight quarts
Container E: forty quarts
Container F: sixty-two quarts

?

Five of the containers hold orange juice,
and one container holds apple juice.

Two customers come into the market and
the first customer buys two containers of orange
juice. The second customer buys twice as
much orange juice as the first customer.
Which container is holding the apple juice?

?

You have a spool with 100 meters of wire.
You need 100 lengths of wire that are one-meter
long each. If it takes you one second to measure
and cut each meter, how long will it take you
to come up with 100 pieces of wire?

?

103

Bill, Tricia, and Beth are siblings, but they differ greatly
in their heights. Tricia is fourteen inches taller
than Beth. The difference between Tricia and Bill is
two inches less than between Bill and Beth.
At 6' 6" Tricia is the tallest. How tall are Bill and Beth?

104

Trent, Mary, and Shawn all work in a factory. Trent earns half of what Mary makes. Shawn earns three times what Trent makes. If the three of them together earn $144 a day, how much are each of them making in a day?

?

105

If ten hens can produce fifteen eggs in a week, how many eggs can fifteen hens produce in two weeks?

106

Using a garden hose, how can you measure out one liter of water if you only have a three-liter and a five-liter jug?

Chris is thirty-three years old today. This is three
times as old as Paul was when Chris was the age that
Paul is today. How old is Paul?

A certain book costs $12 more in hardcover than in
paperback. If the paperback price is two-thirds of the hardcover
price, how much does the book cost in hardcover?

George takes the subway to work each day. He gets on
the subway at the first stop and usually takes a nap.
George falls asleep when the subway still has twice as
far to go as it has already gone. Midway through the ride,
George wakes up to check his watch. When he starts
to doze off again, the subway still has half the distance
to go that it has already traveled. George wakes up
at the end of the ride and goes to work.
What portion of the ride did George sleep through?

Justine is planning to drive across the country.
She is going to drive a few miles on the first day and
add twenty more miles on each subsequent day.
The total trip is going to take her 1,080 miles.
How many miles will she drive on the last day?

?

111

Five retirees meet every week for a game of bridge.
They use a table with six chairs. If they choose a
different seating arrangement each week and
exhaust every possibility, how long have
the retirees played bridge together?

?

Tim and Greg are roofers. Tim makes $100 a day and Greg makes $75 a day. If they just finished a roofing job in which they billed the customer $1,000 for labor, how many days did they work on the roof?

?

113

A jeweler is producing gold rings. For every eleven rings he makes, he has enough scrap gold to be melted into one extra ring. How many rings can he make from the scrap after making 250 gold rings?

A giant gumball machine has seventy-one gumballs left. The flavors are lemon, raspberry, orange, and grape. There are twice as many lemon gumballs as raspberry ones. There is one less orange-flavored gumball than raspberry-flavored, and there are six fewer grape gumballs than lemon ones. How many gumballs do you have to take from the machine to have at least two of one flavor?

At the Fulton Street Fish Market, one sturgeon weighs 120 pounds, and one swordfish weighs thirty-six pounds. What is the weight of one halibut and one grouper, when the grouper and the swordfish together weigh as much as the sturgeon and the halibut?

?

116

It is noon at Grand Central Station when Charlie asks the ticket seller when the next train to Connecticut leaves. He is told the next train leaves when the minute hand and the hour hand of the station clock will be exactly lined up with each other again. How much time does Charlie have before the next train leaves?

?

Mary Ellen has seven people at her birthday
party and everyone wants a piece of cake.
How can Mary Ellen cut the cake into eight pieces
if she's only allowed to make three straight cuts
and she can't move the pieces as she cuts them?

118

Is it possible to put six X's on a Tic Tac Toe board without making three-in-a-row in any direction?

119

In farmer Jack's field, it takes ten cows twenty days to eat all the grass. If fifteen cows are in the field, the grass will be gone in ten days. When will the grass be gone if there are twenty-five cows in the field?

?

120

Using a budget of $100, Jim needs to buy
100 staplers for his company. He has to buy exactly
100 staplers and he must use the entire $100.
If the jumbo staplers cost $6, the regular staplers
cost $3, and the tiny staplers cost 10¢,
how many of each does Jim have to buy?

121

Laura went back-to-school shopping and spent
half her money on a new jacket. She then spent half
of that amount on a pair of sneakers.
If she has $25 left, how much did she spend?

At the hardware store, you can buy nails in boxes of six, nine, and twenty. What is the largest number of nails that it is not possible to obtain by purchasing some combination of boxes?

?

123

A box contains two coins. One coin is heads on both sides and the other is heads on one side and tails on the other. One coin is selected from the box at random and the face of one side is observed. If the face is heads, what is the probability that the other side is heads?

?

124

Using just a four-minute hourglass and a seven-minute hourglass, how can you measure nine minutes?

125

Eric has six coins in his pocket worth a total of $1.15. He can't make change for a dollar, a half dollar, a quarter, a dime, or a nickel. What coins does he have in his pocket?

126

Bill and Mick are both collectors of Bedouin rifles. If Bill were to sell Mick seven rifles, then Bill would have exactly as many rifles as Mick. On the other hand, if Mick were to sell Bill seven rifles, then Bill would have exactly twice as many rifles as Mick. How many rifles does each person have?

?

Robert can eat 100 peanuts in half a minute,
and Matthew can eat half as many in twice the length
of time. How many peanuts can Robert and
Matthew eat in fifteen seconds?

?

128

Terry and Dan were telling their friend the results of a horse race. There were three horses in the race, Quick Ted, Atomic Angie, and Dragonlady. Terry told his friend that Quick Ted had won the race and Atomic Angie came in second. Dan told his friend that Dragonlady had won the race and Quick Ted had come in second.

In reality, however, neither Terry or Dan had told their friend the actual results of the race. Each of them had given one correct statement and one false statement. In what order did the three horses actually finish?

?

133

Yolanda, Erin, and Dan joined a local bird-watching
club and went to the park to look for birds. Each of
them saw one bird that neither of the others did.
Each pair saw one bird that the third did not.
One bird was seen by all three. Of the birds Yolanda
saw, two were yellow. Of the birds Erin saw, three were
yellow. Of the birds Dan saw, four were yellow.
How many yellow birds were seen in all?

Darren, Tom, Rob, and Matt went to a black-tie benefit. When they arrived, they checked their coats, hats, gloves, and canes at the door (each of the gentlemen had one of each). When they checked out, there was a mix up, and each of the men ended up with exactly one article of clothing belonging to each one of the four. Darren and Tom ended up with their own coats, Rob ended up with his own hat, and Matt ended up with his own gloves. Darren did not end up with Rob's cane. Whose coat, hat, gloves, and cane did each of the gentlemen end up with?

135

Troy is an explosives expert who is wiring a cave to explode. He has forty-five minutes to get out of the cave before it blows up, but he doesn't have a watch. All he has are two fuses, each of which will burn up in exactly one hour. They are not of the same length and width as each other, so he can't measure a half hour by noting when one fuse is half burned. Using these two fuses, how can Troy measure forty-five minutes?

?

136

A spider eats three flies a day. Until the spider fills his quota, a fly has a fifty-percent chance of survival if he attempts to pass the web. Assuming five flies have already made the attempt to pass, what is the probability that the sixth fly will survive the attempt?

137

An office has twenty-seven employees.
If there are seven more women than men in the office,
how many employees are women?

?

Jerry goes to the mall to buy a mouse, keyboard, and speakers for his computer. After some shopping around, he finds the best deals for each. The sum of the price of the speakers and six times the cost of the mouse minus three times the cost of the keyboard is seventeen dollars. Also, four times the cost of the keyboard minus twice the cost of the speakers plus seven times the cost of the mouse is thirteen dollars. In addition, seventeen times the cost of the keyboard plus thirty times the cost the mouse minus eight times the cost of the speakers equals sixty-three dollars. How much did Jerry spend at the mall?

?

Eric has $100 more than Ron. After Eric spends twenty dollars on groceries, Eric has five times as much money as Ron. How much money does Ron have?

Nico purchased a camera, a ruler, and an
ice cream bar for $53. He paid $52 more for the
camera than the ice cream bar, and the ruler
cost twice as much as the ice cream bar.
What did he pay for each?

There are enough gumballs in a bag to give twelve gumballs to each of the twenty children, with no gumballs left over. If five children do not want any gumballs, how many gumballs can be given to each of the others?

?

142

A subway car passes an average of three stations every ten minutes. At this rate, how many stations will it pass in one hour?

?

143

Imagine that you have three boxes, one containing two black marbles, one containing two white marbles, and the third, one black marble and one white marble. The boxes were labeled for their contents—BB, WW, and BW—but someone has switched the labels so that every box is now incorrectly labeled. You are allowed to take one marble at a time out of any box, without looking inside, and by this process of sampling you are to determine the contents of all three boxes. What is the smallest number of drawings needed to do this?

A rancher is given $100 to buy 100 animals. She must spend all $100 and have no change left over. Cows cost $10, pigs cost $5, and chickens cost 50¢ apiece. How many of each animal does she have to buy to spend all $100 and have exactly 100 animals?

145

The stock of IBM has been selling for the last year in the range of $70–$80. A year ago the price of IBM was less than or equal to the price of its competitor, Microsoft. Microsoft is now selling at exactly one-eighth of a point below its price last year, but IBM has declined so far it is only two-thirds the price of Microsoft now. What are the two currently selling at?

At Franklin High School, ten percent of
the students use an illegal drug. A drug test yields the
correct result ninety percent of the time, whether
or not the student uses drugs. A random student
is asked to take the drug test and the result is positive.
What is the probability that he uses drugs?

147

A casino uses only \$5 and \$8 chips on its standard roulette wheel. What is the largest wager that cannot be placed?

One shoe weighs eight ounces. One umbrella
is equal to one book plus one shoe. Five books are
equal to one umbrella plus one shoe. One hat is
equal to one umbrella plus one book. How much do
the umbrella, book, and hat each weigh?

149

During his five turns with the cue, a pool player sank 100 balls. During each turn, he sank six more balls than he did during his previous turn. Can you figure out how many balls he sank during each of his five turns?

150

A company flew its employees to Las Vegas for the weekend. Some of the employees decided to go to a nightclub. The cover charge at the nightclub was $10 for men and $6.50 for women. Although there were more men than women at the club, the percentage of men who did not go was twice the percentage of women who did not go. Knowing this percentage and the total number of employees, one can deduce the total cover charge paid by the group. If there were between 60 and 100 employees in Las Vegas, how many went to the club?

151

In a regular nine-inning baseball game, what is
the minimum number of pitches that a pitcher,
who works the whole game, can throw?
Is the pitcher on the home team or the visiting team?
The visitors bat first. The answer is neither
twenty-seven nor twenty-four.

152

What is the fewest number of coins required
to have the exact change for all possible items
that cost from one cent up to and including
one dollar in one-cent increments?

A man is standing on a hill overlooking a calm lake.
His eyes are 100 meters above the surface of the lake.
He sees a balloon in the sky. He finds that the angle
of elevation of the balloon is thirty degrees,
and the angle of depression of the balloon's reflection
in the lake is sixty degrees. What is the height of
the balloon above the lake?

A half-kilometer-long train enters a tunnel that is ten kilometers long. If the train is traveling at thirty-five kilometers per hour, how long will it take for the entire train to pass through the tunnel?

Chris, Leila, Nico, and José are members of the Metropolitan Club. Every pair of members is together on one, and only one, committee in the club. Each committee has three members. What is the smallest possible total membership, and how many committees are there?

156

A store raised the price of their plasma TVs by twenty-five percent for the holidays. After the shopping season was over, they lowered the price by twenty-five percent. Is the price of the TV lower than before, the same, or higher?

?

Jason starts his own online business selling pool tables, and he wants to hire Federal Express to ship the pool tables. FedEx has two trucks that can handle a pool table, one large and one small. Their large truck is twice as high, twice as wide, and twice as long as their small one. FedEx has decided to charge $500 per shipment for each delivery they make with a fully loaded small truck. Assuming that charges are based on each truck's volume, what should FedEx charge for each delivery they make with a fully-loaded large truck?

A teacher brings in a bag of lollipops for her students. John takes three-fifths of the lollipops and Bill has three-fourths of Paul's share of the remaining lollipops. What fraction of the total number of lollipops does Paul have?

159

A poll was taken at a local town hall meeting to see what newspapers the citizens were reading. Sixty-four percent were reading the *Sun-Times*, twenty-two percent were reading the *Post*, and seven percent were reading both. What percentage of the citizens polled were reading no newspaper?

?

Ira was selling air conditioners during a five-day heat wave. He sold thirty air conditioners total, and each day he sold three more air conditioners than the day before. How many air conditioners did he sell the first day?

?

161

There are 100 contestants at a beauty pageant
and each contestant is either a blonde or a brunette.
Given any two of the contestants, at least one
is a blonde. How many of the contestants are
blondes and how many are brunettes?

?

Jenny is trying to figure out the weight of
a wheel of cheese. She knows that one-fifth
of a pound of cheese is perfectly balanced by
two-fifths of a wheel of the same cheese. How
much does the entire wheel of cheese weigh?

?

163

A farmer is trying to fill a small pond on his land so the livestock can drink. He hires two companies to fill the pond. One company can fill the pond in two hours, and another company can fill it in five hours. However, the ground soaks up the entire pond in six hours. With both companies filling the pond and the ground soaking up the water, how long will it take to fill the pond?

?

164

At a company's Christmas party, one-third
of the employees left early. Later on in the evening,
two-fifths of the remaining employees left, and a few
hours later, two-thirds of the remaining employees
went home. If there are six employees still
at the party, how many attended?

?

165

A box of chocolates can be divided equally among three, five, or thirteen people. What is the smallest number of chocolates the box can contain?

?

Delivery man Wayne gets paid $500 for every delivery he makes on time. The only problem is, he has to speed to make the delivery on time. He gets pulled over for speeding twenty-five percent of the time. This makes him late for the delivery, which means he doesn't get paid, and he has to pay a $200 speeding ticket. How much is Wayne making on average per delivery?

?

Fernando is studying a type of bacteria that multiplies every minute. He places one bacteria strain in a Petri dish, and after one minute the bacteria splits. One minute later, the two bacteria split again. One minute after that, the four bacteria split, and so on. After three hours, the dish is halfway full. How much longer will it take to fill the dish completely?

168

Four friends decide to go out to the movies.
When they arrive, there are four empty seats in
the theater. How many different ways can the four
friends combine to fill the seats?

?

169

If everyone on the South Side of Chicago owns an even number of cars, no one owns more than 100 cars, and no two people own the same number of cars, what is the maximum number of cars on the South Side?

170

Freckles the clown has just learned how to juggle four balls. How many throws must he make before the balls are returned to their original positions?

Freckles starts out with two balls in each hand and throws one ball from one hand, then another ball from the second hand, then the remaining ball from the first hand, and so on. Except for the first throw for each hand, there is a moment where the throwing hand no longer holds anything after each throw.

?

171

With the price of cigarettes skyrocketing, Danny
figured out that if he collected cigarette butts,
he could make a cigarette from every five butts
found. He found twenty-five butts, so how
many cigarettes could he smoke?

?

At Stanford University, there are 4,215 freshmen,
3,401 sophomores, 1,903 juniors, and 1,757 seniors.
One student will randomly be chosen to
receive an award. What percent chance is
there that it will be a junior?

Albert, Bob, and Carl are eating at an all-you-can-eat buffet. Albert makes 2.4 times as many trips to the buffet as Bob, and Bob makes six fewer trips than Carl. What is the smallest possible total number of trips the three makes to the buffet, assuming that each person makes at least one trip?

?

Michael was training for a race by running up and down
a hill. It took him sixty minutes to run up the two-mile
hill and forty minutes to run down it. How long would it
take Michael to run one mile on a flat surface?

?

175

All of the students at a high school are playing baseball, football, or both. Seventy-three percent of the students are baseball players, and sixty-two percent are football players. If there are 200 students, how many of them are playing both baseball and football?

Each child in the Smith family has at least three brothers and four sisters. What is the smallest number of children the Smith family might have?

Dominic and his brother can build a wall five
bricks long and five bricks high in one minute.
How long will it take them to build a wall
ten bricks long and ten bricks high?

?

178

Gary and Jim each have a collection of matchbox cars.
Gary says that if Jim will give him nine cars, they will
have an equal number; but if Gary will give Jim nine of
his cars, Jim will have four times as many cars as Gary.
How many matchbox cars does Jim have?

?

Rochester and Syracuse are eighty-eight miles apart.
If Eric leaves Rochester on a bicycle traveling ten miles
per hour and Alison leaves Syracuse on foot, traveling
one mile per hour, how many miles will Eric have
to travel before meeting Alison on the way?

180

Joan spent one-fourth of her life as a girl, one-eighth as a youth, and one-half as an adult. If Joan spent ten years as an old woman, how old is she?

?

181

At the playground, there are ten bicycles and tricycles.
If the total number of wheels is twenty-four,
how many tricycles are there?

?

182

If it takes five dolphins five minutes to eat
five fish, how many minutes would it take
four dolphins to eat four fish?

?

183

An upholsterer is putting new fabric on the back of a chair. The size of the fabric is 27" x 27." The upholsterer uses tacks all along the edges of the square so that there are twenty-eight tacks on each side of the square. Each tack is the same distance from the neighboring tacks. How many tacks in all does the upholsterer use?

There are two flagpoles on the military base. One pole is sixteen-feet tall and casts a shadow four-feet long on the ground. The second flagpole is sixty-four feet tall. How long would the shadow on the second flagpole be?

?

185

Erin, a teacher at the local elementary school, likes to use chalk. She just bought a pack of sixteen sticks. When a stick is three-quarters gone, it gets too small for her to use, so she stops using it. When she has enough of these small pieces to make another stick of the original size, she joins them together and adds them back into the box as a new stick. If Erin uses one piece of chalk each day, how many days would her box of sixteen last?

?

Tim owns a mason company, and was hired to build a brick house. The entire house can be built in thirty-one days with five masons. Ten days after they started building the house, Tim hired ten more masons to get the house built quicker. How many more days are required to finish the house?

?

Stephen just finished all four final exams for
the semester. He found out that his average score was
eighty-one. He also found out that his average in
Physics and Math was seventy-eight. What was his
average score for English and History?

188

The backgammon world championship took place
in Monte Carlo. The tournament was organized in
a round-robin format, with every participant
playing a match against every other player once.
If 105 matches were played in total, how many
players were there in the tournament?

189

The family dog, Buster, weighs eighty pounds more than Felix, the cat. If their combined weight is 120 pounds, how much does Buster weigh?

?

Jess's family sent her to summer camp. In the mornings, she would run and in the evenings she would play softball. She only did one thing each day, however, and there were a few days when she decided to do nothing at all. There were thirteen mornings when she did nothing, eleven evenings when she didn't play softball, and a total of sixteen days when she either ran or played softball. How long was Jess at camp?

191

The local factory's workforce is twenty percent part-time workers, with the rest of the workers full-time. At the end of the year, thirty percent of the full-time workers received bonuses. If seventy-two full-time workers received bonuses, how many workers does the factory employ?

?

Two rival colleges decided on a tug of war. From their
starting positions, College A pulls College B forward
three meters, and is then pulled forward themselves five
meters. College B then pulls College A forward two
meters. If the first college to be pulled forward
ten meters loses, how many more meters must
College B pull College A forward to win?

?

Jonathan finds that by wearing different combinations of the jackets, shirts, and pairs of pants that he owns, he can create ninety different outfits. If he owns five jackets and three pairs of pants, how many shirts does he own?

194

Josh and Brian are both champion archers.
They decide to put a target 100-yards away and
see who can hit the center first. They decide to
alternate shots until someone hits the bull's-eye.
It is so far away, though, that they only hit the
target half the time. If Josh shoots first, what
are the odds of him winning the contest?

A fog horn sounds regularly five times a minute. A neighboring fog horn blows regularly four times a minute. If they blow simultaneously, after how many seconds will they blow together again?

196

The Cullinan Diamond is the largest diamond in the world. A group of twelve thieves stole it from the Queen of England. During the getaway, however, they dropped the diamond, and it broke into seven equal pieces. They took the seven pieces to a jeweler and asked him to divide them evenly, so each of the twelve thieves gets an equal amount. How did the jeweler divide the pieces?

197

A ship is sitting in port and the crew hangs a rope ladder over the side so the people can get on and off the ship. If the tide rises one inch per hour, at the end of five hours how much of the ladder will be remaining above water, assuming that ten feet were above water when the tide began to rise?

198

If today is Thursday, what is the day that
follows the day that comes after the day that
precedes the day before yesterday?

?

199

A man went to an auction and bought a wolf, a goat, and a bag of grain. When he leaves the auction, he starts walking home. To get home, he must cross a river, but he's only allowed to take one item across the bridge with him at a time. If he leaves the wolf with the goat, the wolf will eat the goat. If the goat is left alone with the grain, the goat will eat the grain. How can the man cross the river without any of his possessions being eaten?

200

Alison owes Robert $4, Robert owes Christine $3, and Carol owes Alison $5. If Christine settles all the debts by giving money to both Alison and Robert, how much will she give Alison?

?

201

During the Little League baseball season every
team plays every other team in the league ten times.
If there are ten teams in the league, how many games
are played in the league in one season?

?

ANSWERS

1. Peter wins again. Peter is the faster runner and he can run the extra five meters faster than Bill.

2. Billy sold the card twice, for $10 and $8. He paid $15 for the card so he came out ahead by $3.

3. Twenty-five lollipops costing 25¢ each. $6.25 equals 625¢. And 625 divided by 25 = 25.

4. Twelve months. When one person is host, three other people could be the snack provider. Each person gets a chance to be host for three months, each month with a different snack provider. In total, there are twelve different host/snack combinations.

5. It would be more cost effective to get the rust-proofing done. Without the rust-proofing the cost is $17.50 per wheel per year and with the rust-proofing the cost is $16.66 per wheel per year.

6. Adam got there first using his bicycle.

7. They are both making the same amount. Let's say that on their first year they both earn $10,000. In year two, Alison gets a raise to $11,000 and Eric's pay drops to $9,000. In year three, Alison's pay drops by ten percent and goes to $9,900 while Eric's pay rises ten percent and goes from $9,000 to $9,900. They are both now earning $9,900 a year.

8. The first shooter has a two-thirds chance of hitting his opponent first.

9. Beth.

10. Dropping it in the rowboat. Since the marble is denser than water, dropping it into the rowboat will raise the water level higher. Try substituting a marble for a fully-inflated balloon. If you managed to push the balloon underwater it would raise the water level considerably higher than if you dropped the balloon into the rowboat.

11. $1.19. Three quarters, four dimes, four pennies.

12. They played eleven games. John lost three games. He had to win three additional games to break even. Then he had to win five more games to win $50. 3 + 3 + 5 = 11.

13. Nine times. 1:23, 2:34, 3:45, 4:56, 9:10, 10:11, 11:12, 12:13, 12:34.

14. None. 4 + 8 + 12 + 16 + 20 = 60. Because this total is the exact number of pies sold, there could not have been any pies sold on the first day.

15. Forty jellybeans in the jar.

16. One gold bar weighs five kilograms. By removing one gold bar from each side of the scale, two gold bars weigh ten kilograms total.

17. Steve must give Lisa five marbles. He would then have five less, she would have five more for a difference of ten.

18. Six.

19. The only matching colors available for Louisa's present is red paper and a red bow. The only contrasting paper color remaining for Samantha's present is silver. Maria's present is left with green paper and a gold bow.

20. Cut four of the apples into three pieces each, and then cut the three remaining apples into four pieces each.

21. Twenty-nine days. The doubling still occurs each day; we can just rule out the first day since it was doubled initially.

22. Three sons and four daughters

23. One hour and five minutes.

24. Seven. Jess has none and Courtney has one.

25. She started with $100.

26. One. Consider jar #1. Over all possible permutations (N=9!), there is a one-in-nine chance that this jar gets its correct label. Same result concerning each of the eight jars #2, 3, 4,...9. In total, there are 9 × N/9 = N jars correctly labeled; that means (N-correctly-labeled-jars/N-possible-configurations) = 1 jar is labeled correctly on average.

27. Ninety-nine. With only one winner, there must be ninety-nine losers, requiring ninety-nine matches.

28. Twenty cents.

29. The weight will rise.

30. Seven. To average two hours a day over six days, Jimmy must practice 2 × 6, or twelve hours. From Monday through Friday, he practices five hours—one hour each day. To total twelve hours, he must practice 12–5, or seven hours, on Saturday.

31. $160 dollars. The easy way to solve this is to divide 320 in half, since the half of the seventy-nine percent that tipped two dollars is the same as the full seventeen percent tipping one dollar.

32. Trish has three handbags, one gold, one brown, and one white.

33. Twelve jellybeans. Ally ate half the remaining jellybeans plus three more to leave none, so she must have eaten six jellybeans. Tommy ate half the jellybeans and left six, meaning there were twelve to start.

34. Five cars. $1,500 × 5 = $7,500 profit.

35. Ten games. Craig won the first three, and Dan had to win the next seven in order to win $4.

36. John is the tallest, then Bill, then Mick.

37. Kelly is eight years older than Danielle.

38. She lost $100.

39. Enriqué is sleeping between Ricardo and Juan.

40. $116.

41. Toby made each person ride another person's horse. This would ensure that everyone would want to come in first so they wouldn't lose.

42. It only passes ten times.

43. Yes. She has seven daughters.

44. Stephen started with $62.

45. Eleven. Trains pass by every half hour for nine total, plus two pulling into the cities.

46. Thirty-one runners total. Since the track is a closed circuit, we simply add 1/5 + 5/6 = 31/30. 30 runners plus Joseph.

47. Ten kids.

48. France.

49. Eleven tires total. 4,000 miles × 4 tires = 16,000 total miles. 1,500 × 11 = 16,500 total miles.

50. Six pairs. Five pairs will only get her fifty miles and both marathons are fifty-two miles.

51. Total cost of meal is $60. 3 people × $20 = $60. Eight dishes have been eaten, therefore each dish costs $7.50. Blake brought 5 dishes x $7.50 = $37.50 minus his $20 share or $17.50. Brian brought 3 dishes × $7.50 minus his share = $2.50.

52. Eight chickens and Fourteen goats.

53. Twenty-seven rungs.

54. She should take the first job. In two years, it will have paid $56,000, while the second job will have paid only $55,000.

55. They must charge four dollars per serving to make a 100 percent profit.

56. Eric can reach the summit using only two Sherpas. The three of them leave base camp, each with four days' worth of food. At the end of the first day, they all have three days' worth of food left. The first Sherpa leaves two days' worth of food with Eric and the other Sherpa, and heads back to base camp with one days' worth of food in his pack. On the second day, the last Sherpa heads back to base camp after leaving one days' worth of food with Eric. Eric now has four days' worth of food and only four days left to get to the summit. He will die of starvation on the way down, however.

57. Fifty-nine cents. Ten seven-cent coins minus the eleven-cent coin.

58. Ten $1 bills, 100 $5 bills, nine $10 bills, and eighteen $50 bills.

59. Courtney has six pennies, six nickels, six dimes, and six quarters.

60. Her average speed is 6.7 miles per hour. It takes Elena two hours to run the first ten miles and one hour to run the last ten miles, meaning she needs three hours to run the total of twenty miles.

61. Label the sacks from 1 to 5. Take one coin out of sack 1, and label it 1. Take two coins out of sack 2, and label them both with a 2. Take three coins out of sack 3, and label each with a 3. Continue this pattern with sacks 4 and 5. Put these fifteen coins on the tray of the scale. If all fifteen weighed one pound, the scale would register fifteen pounds, but since one or more of the coins weighs only nine-tenths of a pound, the scale will register less than fifteen. Subtract the number on the scale from fifteen. Your answer will tell you the number of the sack with the lighter coins. (If the scale registers 14.8 pounds, it's sack 2. If the

scale registers 14.5 pounds, it's sack 5.)

62. Bernie had the best average. Derek batted 73.3 percent, and Bernie batted 75 percent.

63. Ten blocks.

64. They both drank the same amount of caffeine.

65. Alison has one cat and one goldfish.

66. The time is 8:30.

67. You still only need seventeen bakers.

68. There are four possibilities:
One spoon and one fork.
Two spoons.
One fork and one spoon.
Two forks.
In three of the four possibilities, you'll wind

up with at least one spoon. So the chances of picking at least one spoon are three in four or, in another phrasing, three to one.

69. If you add up all the losses, you find that 100 students lost a total of 310 items. That total means that, at a minimum, 100 students lost three items, and ten (the remainder when dividing 310 by 100) must have lost all four items.

70. Coco, Rocky, Winston, Fluffy, and Lulu.

71. Ten cookies.

72. Jackie had $6 before she found the $4.

73. Either forty pennies, eighty nickels, and two dimes, or forty-five pennies, two nickels, two dimes, and one quarter.

74. Eight days. The snail makes one foot of progress every twenty-four hours. So after seven days, he will have climbed seven feet. Then on day eight, he will climb the three feet he manages per day and gets out of the well.

75. 420 students: This is the only number under 500 that can be divided evenly by 3, 4, 5, and 7.

76. Beth is twenty-two years old.

77. Four flies (twenty-four legs) and three spiders (twenty-four legs). No other combination will work.

78. Andy has gone through eight times, Bill four times, Chris eleven times, Drake six times, Eric three times.

79. From youngest to oldest, the six brothers are ten, fourteen, eighteen, twenty-two, twenty-six, and thirty.

80. If you want one dollar in twenty-eight coins, I should give you three quarters and twenty-five pennies.

81. Four people can make twelve hats in six hours.

82. Five pieces of candy at 10¢, one piece of candy at 3¢, ninety-four pieces of candy at 2 pieces for 1¢ equals $1.

83. Bill took eleven lessons.

84. Six shoes. If she takes out five shoes, she could have one of each color, with no two matching colors.

85. John spent $2,500 and $4,500 for a total of $7,000. John sold the painting for $3,500 and $5,500 for a total of $9,000. John came out ahead by $2,000.

86. $260. Sally makes $280. If Jerry makes $50 more than this, then Jerry must make $280 + $50 or $330. Dan makes $70 less than this amount, or $260.

87. Juanita solved eighteen puzzles correctly, earning thirty-six points. She failed to solve twelve correctly, losing thirty-six points.

88. The rain gauge was half-filled on Saturday. It doubled on Sunday, to become completely filled.

89. 33.3 percent. If the car originally cost $30,000, with the twenty-five percent deduction, it would cost $22,500. To bring the price back to the original $30,000, you'd have to add $7,500, which is one-third of $22,500, or 33.3 percent.

90. If you want one dollar in six coins, I should give you three quarters, two dimes, and one nickel.

91. He should buy the ring from the first jewelry store. Hypothetically, if Brian proposed twice, Andrea should say yes once and no once. This would mean that if he bought the ring from the first store twice he would have spent $6,600 and if he bought the ring from the second store twice he would have spent $7,000. On average, the ring would cost him $3,300 from the first store and $3,500 from the second one.

92. The British diplomat would get assassinated 5 times (50% × 10) and the French diplomat would get assassinated 1.5 times (25% × 6). Therefore, the British diplomat is in greater danger.

93. Seven rows. eight oranges in the bottom row, two in the top.

94. Sixty feet.

95. There are four players on each team.

96. Four hours.

97. The five football players will win. If there were only four football players on one side and two soccer players on the other side, it would be a tie.

98. Eighty miles.

99. Ralph. Tommy is selling the shoes for $63.75 and Ralph is selling them for $63.

100. Carlos picked fifteen.

101. Container E holds the apple juice. The second customer can buy twice as much as the first customer if the first customer buys Containers A and C (for a total of sixty-six quarts) and the second customer buys Containers B, D, and F (for a total of 132 quarts). The remaining container, E, must hold the apple juice.

102. Ninety-nine seconds. Each cut, including the 99th, produces two pieces of wire.

103. Beth is 5' 4" and Bill is 6'.

104. Trent makes $24, Mary makes $48, Shawn makes $72.

105. Forty-five eggs.

106. Fill the three-liter jug and pour it into the five-liter jug. Fill the three-liter jug again and add the water to the same five-liter jug, filling it to the top. What's left in the three-liter jug is one liter of water.

107. Twenty-two years old.

108. $36

109. George slept through half the trip.

110. She drives 200 miles on the last day. If n = miles traveled in one day, let each subsequent day be n + 20 (the daily increase in miles). With this you'll find that she would have to have traveled forty miles the first day, sixty the second day, 100 on the fourth day, and 200 on the ninth and final day. This is the only way it would add up to 1080.

111. They've been playing for 720 weeks or 13.8 years. The number of possible seating arrangements is 6 × 5 × 4 × 3 × 2, which is 720.

112. 1,000 divided by $175 is 5.7, so they worked on the roof for six days.

113. Twenty-four additional gold rings.

114. Twenty-seven gumballs.

115. The grouper weighs 102 pounds. The weight of the halibut is given indirectly by saying two halibut weigh the same as one swordfish. One grouper and two halibut are equal to the weight of one sturgeon and one halibut. One grouper and one halibut must have the same weight as one sturgeon. So, the grouper is 120 pounds minus eighteen pounds, or 102 pounds.

116. Charlie has twenty-one minutes and forty-nine seconds.

117. Use two cuts to make an X so that you have four

pieces, then make a horizontal cut through the cake to make eight pieces.

118. Yes.
XXO
XOX
OXX

119. Twenty-five cows would eat all the grass in five days.

120. One jumbo stapler, twenty-nine regular staplers, and seventy tiny staplers.

121. $75.

122. Forty-three nails.

123. Two-thirds.

124. Flip both hourglasses over. When the four-minute hourglass runs out, flip it back over immediately. When the seven-minute hourglass runs out, flip that back over immediately, too. One minute later, the four-minute hourglass will run out again. At this point, flip the seven-minute hourglass back over. The seven-minute hourglass has only been running for a minute, so when it is flipped over again it will only run for a minute more before running out. When it does, exactly nine minutes will have passed.

125. A half dollar, a quarter, and four dimes.

126. Bill had forty-nine rifles and Mick had thirty-five.

127. 62.5 peanuts.

128. Dragonlady won, Atomic Angie came in second, and Quick Ted came in third.

129. Two half-full barrels are dumped into one of the empty barrels. Two more half-full barrels are dumped into another one of the empty barrels. This results in nine full barrels, three half-full barrels, and nine empty barrels. Each son gets three full barrels, one half-full barrel, and three empty barrels.

130. Take a piece of fruit from the box marked "cherries and strawberries." If the fruit you take is a cherry, then that box must be the box containing just cherries. Therefore, the box marked "strawberries" can't be the box containing just cherries, and it can't be the box containing just strawberries either, so it must be the box containing cherries and strawberries. The remaining box is therefore the box containing just strawberries.

131. Ask one of the men what the other man would answer to the question, "Is the door on the left the correct door?" Then assume the answer you are given is false and act on that knowledge. If the man you ask is the liar, he'll incorrectly give you the truthful man's answer. If the man you ask is the truthful man, he'll correctly give you the liar's wrong answer.

132. Say It Fast came in first. Lion Heart and Sir Oscar tied for second place. Silver Wagon came in fourth. Master David came in fifth.

133. Five yellow birds were seen.

134. Darren had his own coat, Tom's hat, Rob's gloves, and Matt's cane. Tom had his own coat, Matt's hat, Darren's gloves, and Rob's cane. Rob had Matt's coat, his own hat, Tom's gloves, and Darren's cane. Matt had Rob's coat, Darren's hat, his own gloves, and Tom's cane.

135. Light one fuse at both ends and, at the same time, light the second fuse at one end. When the first fuse has completely burned, a half hour has elapsed and the second fuse has a half hour left to go. At this time, light the second fuse from the other end. This will cause it to burn out in fifteen more minutes. At that point, exactly

forty-five minutes will have elapsed.

136. Three-quarters.

137. Seventeen. You just need to find two numbers, seven apart, that add up to 27. With trial and error you should be able to find them soon—ten and seventeen; there must be seventeen women working at the office.

138. Jerry spent $22. The speakers cost $14. The keyboard costs $5. And the mouse costs $3.

139. Twenty dollars.

140. Camera: $52.25. Ruler: 50¢. Ice cream bar: 25¢.

141. Sixteen. Find the total number of gumballs in the bag, then divide by the new number of children who will be sharing them.

142. Eighteen stations. The subway will pass 60/10 or six times as many stations in one hour as it passes in ten minutes. In ten minutes, it passes three stations; in sixty minutes, it must pass 6 × 3, or eighteen stations.

143. You can learn the contents of all three boxes by drawing just one marble. The key to the solution is your knowledge that the labels on all three of the boxes are incorrect. You must draw a marble from the box labeled "black-white." Assume that the marble drawn is black. You know then that the other marble in this box must be black also, otherwise the label would

be correct. Since you have now identified the box containing two black marbles, you can at once tell the contents of the box marked "white-white." you know it cannot contain two white marbles, because its label has to be wrong; it cannot contain two black marbles, because you have identified that box; therefore, it must contain one black and one white marble. The third box, of course, must then be the one holding two white marbles. You can solve the puzzle by the same reasoning if the marble you draw from the "black-white" box happens to be white instead of black.

144. You buy one cow, nine pigs, and ninety chickens.

145. IBM is at 70 and Microsoft is at 105 3/8.

146. Fifty percent.

147. $27.

148. The umbrella weighs twelve ounces, the book four ounces, and the hat sixteen ounces.

149. During his five turns at the table he sank eight, fourteen, twenty, twenty-six, and thirty-two balls.

150. There were twenty-six men and twenty women, or forty-six altogether at the club.

151. Twenty-five pitches. Twenty-four pitches that result in outs and one for a home run to end the game. The pitcher would be on the visiting team.

152. A total of nine coins are needed. Four pennies, one nickel, two dimes, one quarter, and one half-dollar.

153. The balloon is 200 meters above the lake.

154. It will take the train eighteen minutes. The front of the train has to initially travel ten kilometers to leave the tunnel, and then a further one-half kilometer until the rear of the train has left the tunnel—a total of ten and one-half kilometers. Which takes 60 × (10.5 / 35) = 18 minutes.

155. Seven members and seven committees.

156. The price of the TV is less than it was before the twenty-five percent increase and the twenty-five percent decrease. If the TV cost $1,000, you know that twenty-five percent of 1,000 is 250. So, after the twenty-five percent increase, the cost was $1,250. Now find twenty-five percent of $1,250. Subtract this amount ($312.50) from $1,250 to find the reduced price. It's $937.50—that's $62.50 less than the original price of $1,000.

157. FedEx should charge $4,000 for a large truck-load. Since each dimension of the large truck (height, width, and length) is twice that of the small truck, the volume of the large truck is eight times that of the small truck. So, for a large truckload, FedEx should charge eight times the price of a small truckload. That's 8 x $500, or $4,000.

158. Paul has 8/35 and Bill has 6/35.

159. Twenty-one percent. 64 + 22 – 7 = 79. 100 – 79 is 21.

160. None.

161. There can only be one brunette; therefore, the other ninety-nine are blondes.

162. It weighs half a pound. 1/5 x 5/2 = 5/10 or half a pound.

163. One and seven-eighths hours.

164. Forty-five.

165. 195.

166. $325 per delivery.

167. One minute. Remember, they double

every minute, so when the dish is half full, it will only take one more doubling to fill it.

168. Twenty-four.

169. Fifty.

170. Eight throws.

171. Six. Danny made five cigarettes from the twenty-five butts, smoked them, and then made an additional cigarette from the five butts that were left from the five that he made.

172. Seventeen percent. Divide the number of juniors (1,903) by the total number of students (11,276).

173. There were twenty-eight total trips made, with Albert making twelve of them, Bob making five, and Carl making eleven.

174. Michael can run one mile on a flat surface in twenty-four minutes. He can run three miles an hour downhill and two miles an hour uphill. If you take the average of the two rates, you find that Michael runs 2.5 miles per hour on a flat surface.

175. Thirty-five percent are playing both for a total of seventy students.

176. The smallest number of children the Smith family might have is nine.

177. Four minutes. The first wall has twenty-five bricks. The second wall has four times as many, so it will take four times as long, or four minutes.

178. Jim has thirty-nine cars.

179. Together they cover the distance at eleven miles per hour so they will cover the distance of eighty-eight miles in eight hours. In eight hours they will meet and Eric will have traveled eighty miles.

180. Joan is eighty years old.

181. There are four tricycles in the park.

182. It would still take five minutes for four dolphins to eat four fish.

183. 108 tacks. The four corners of the square have one tack each, so each side of the square now requires twenty-six tacks. The total number of tacks used = 4 + (4 x 26) = 108.

184. Sixteen feet.
$(64/16) \times 4 = 16$ feet.

185. Twenty-one days. Erin has sixteen pieces in the original box. The small pieces make four new pieces and the small pieces of the four new pieces make one more for twenty-one.

186. Seven days will finish the house.

187. Eighty-four was the average.

Total marks in 4 exams = $4 \times 81 = 324$.
Total marks for Physics and Math = $2 \times 78 = 156$.
Total marks in English and History = $324 - 156 = 168$.
Average marks in English and History = $168/2 = 84$.

188. There are fifteen players in the tournament. $14 + 13 + \ldots + 2 + 1 = 105$.

189. Buster weighs 100 pounds.

190. Jess was at camp for nineteen days.

191. 300. Twenty percent of the workers are part-time, so eighty percent of the workers are full-time. Thirty percent received bonuses and this amounted to seventy-two workers. Thirty percent of eighty percent of total workers (n) equals seventy-two. $3/10 \times 8/10 \times n = 72$, or $24/100 \times n = 72$. Therefore, $n = 72 \times 100/24$ or 300.

192. Six. Find out how far College A has moved thus far. They pulled College B forward three meters, so A moved backward three meters. Then they were pulled forward five meters and then a further two meters. In total then they have moved forward $(-3) + 5 + 2 = 4$ meters. They must be pulled a further six meters to be pulled ten meters forward.

193. Six. For every pair of pants, he can wear five different jackets, giving five different combinations for each pair of pants, or $3 \times 15 = 15$ different combinations of pants and jackets. With each of these combinations he can wear any of his different shirts. The different combinations of shirts, jackets, and pants is (number of shirts) / 15. We are told this equals ninety, so ninety divided by fifteen equals six.

194. Josh has a two-thirds chance of successfully hitting the bull's-eye before Brian does.

195. Sixty. If you convert everything to seconds, the first fog horn blows every twelve seconds and the second fog horn blows every fifteen seconds. Then find the lowest common denominator, which is sixty, and you arrive at the answer.

196. He cut four of the pieces into three pieces each and then cut the three remaining pieces into four pieces each, and divided them accordingly.

197. Ten feet. The ship will rise with the tide and so will the ladder, so it won't affect the amount that is above water.

198. Wednesday.

199. Take the goat across and leave it on the other side. Then go back, get the wolf. Bring the wolf to the other side and take the goat back with you. Take the grain to the other side and leave it there, then go back and get the goat.

200. $1. Christine is owed $3 by Robert, and she owes $5 to Alison. She needs a cash loss of $2 to settle all debts. Alison, on the other hand, is owed $5 by Christine and owes $4 to Robert. She must have a gain of $1. Since Christine settles all debts, this $1 must come from Christine, and this is the answer.

201. 450. In the ten team league, each team plays the other nine teams ten times each. $9 \times 10 = 90$ games per team per season. With ten different teams, we arrive at 900 total games played. Then we divide this by two since there are two teams playing in each game. 900 divided by 2 equals 450.

ABOUT THE AUTHOR

Nathan Haselbauer is the president and founder of the International High IQ Society. He enjoys writing challenging questions, both for fun and for use in intelligence tests. His latest achievement, the Test for Exceptional Intelligence, is one of the most difficult and popular high-ceiling intelligence tests available. He was born in upstate New York and currently lives in New York City.

Also from Fair Winds Press

THE LITTLE BOOK OF BATHROOM PHILOSOPHY
Gregory Bergman
ISBN: 1-59233-075-4
$9.95/£5.99/$13.95 CAN
Paperback; 208 pages
Available wherever books are sold

Learn everything you need to know about deep thinking in just a few trips to the loo!

Join Gregory Bergman on a humorous and easy-to-follow journey through the history of philosophy from Socrates: *And in knowing that you know nothing, that makes you the smartest of all*; to Sartre: *Only the guy who isn't rowing has time to rock the boat*. Along the way you'll hear from Kant: *Science is organized knowledge. Wisdom is organized life*; Dewey: *No man's credit is as good as his money*; and twenty-four other great thinkers.

THE LITTLE BOOK OF BATHROOM MEDITATIONS
Michelle Heller
ISBN: 1-59233-028-2
$9.95/£5.99/$13.95 CAN
Paperback; 208 pages
Available wherever books are sold

Solitude + Privacy + Words of Wisdom = Enlightenment

The bathroom: In our hurried lives, what other place allows us to get away from the rigors of daily life and to be left alone, uninterrupted by phones, kids, or work? The bathroom is where people are most themselves, so there is no better place to meditate on one's self and one's soul.

Filled with quotes, parables, and wise words from history's most brilliant visionaries, *The Little Book of Bathroom Meditations* offers daily inspiration.